What Would It Be Like To Be There

What Would It Be Like To Be There

by Freda Harrison

ARPress
45 Dan Road Suite 15
Canton MA 02021
  Hotline: 1(888) 821-0229
  Fax: 1(508) 545-7580

Ordering Information:
Quantity sales. Special discounts are available on quantity purchases by corporations, associations, and others. For details, contact the publisher at the address above.

Printed in the United States of America.

ISBN-13:   Softcover   979-8-89676-559-2
            eBook   979-8-89676-561-5
            Hardback   979-8-89676-560-8

Library of Congress Control Number: 2026906420

This book is dedicated to my Sweet and Darling Husband and to cancer people out there, May God be with you.

May this book touch your heart.

What would it be like to be there.

JERRY HARRISON JR.

MAY 19, 1953 – JULY 4, 2025 (Age 72)

Also, to our Pastor Rev. Adam Harrison. Who Preached the most amazing sermon at church, the day after my husband's celebration of life service.

What Would It Be Like To Be There

He restoreth my Soul: He Leadeth me in the paths of righteousness for his name's sake.

Yea, though I walk through the valley of the shadow of death, I will fear no evil for thou art with me; thy rod and thy staff they comfort me.

Thou preparest a table before me in the presence of mine enemies: thou anointest my head with oil; my cup runneth over.

Arrangements made with integrity by Shawn Chapman Funeral Home, Crematory, and Monuments.

HEAVEN

A place of Magical beauty that eyes have never seen. A place were Gods word says he went to prepare a place for us and where also will be.

When we get there we will sing a song the angels can't sing amazing grace how sweet does it sound?

We were so blessed to have a blended family he had two children from a previous marriage as well as one son and one daughter: a total of four. All around the same ages.

Freda Harrison

What Would It Be Like To Be There

To be absent in the body is present with the Lord

Oh, the love of God is so amazing, who else can make a pretty little bird give it hundreds of songs to sing, every day, right on time.

Freda Harrison

Picture of The Church

Several years ago, we were watching tv and an elderly lady had no family, and she knew she was close to death. So, she wants to go to funeral home to make her arrangements. All she had was a very nice car. So, she told the funeral home to sell raffle tickets for her car, but they would have to be present at her funeral to win the car because she knew she had no family that no one would be there for her and she would know that her car would go to a good cause. It was a young college student who won the car they interviewed her on tv and asked her why she bought a ticket and came to her funeral and she said the lady's story was so sad and that no one needed to be alone in a time, so she was happy to help.

Honey, you did not have to be alone at your celebration or live the house was full. There were people standing in no seats. I love you so much my darling. God Bless us so much will never be able to thank him enough.

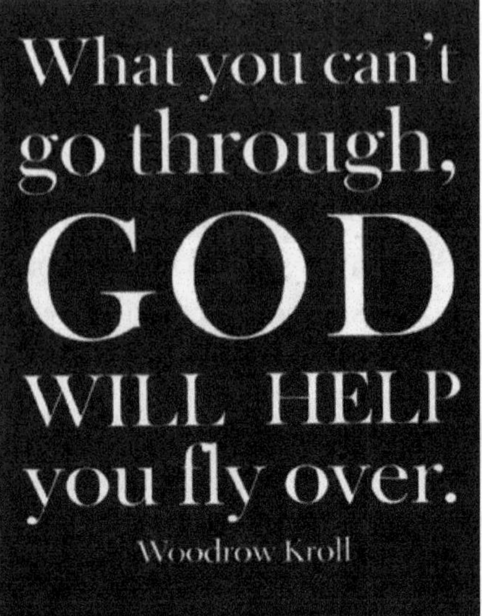

Blessed is the one
who perseveres
under trial because,
having stood the test,
that person will
receive the
crown of life.

13

What Would It Be Like To Be There

Heaven

Some call it paradise

A place of such

Beauty our eyes cannot imagine

Rev 21-22

Walls of Jasper

Streets of Gold

No light will be required because

He will be the light in that big city.

Gentleness
Kindness
Love
Patience
Self-Control
Faithfulness
Generosity
Joy
Peace
This Fruit is Always in Season

The Son of God

Will be the light no sorrow no grief

No pain no sadness no more tears to wipe away

Because he will wipe away every tear from our eyes.

We all will be standing with our Lord and Savior.

How will we be known in Heaven

Corinthians 13:12

We will be know as we are known.

All earthly desires will be gone

And will be transformed into all heavenly bodies

Like unto angles glorified in God

What our bodies will be like in Heaven

18

Matthew 22:30, Mark 12:25 and Luke 20:36

In heaven our bodies will be liking unto an angel
Glorified By God.

Praise God we will be known as we are known.

We will know

Each other as we are known on earth.

To be absent with the body is to present with the
Lord

2 Corinthians 5:4

To all Christians who have been born again and
redeemed by the blood of the lamb.

When you take your last breath on earth is to be
present with the Lord.

It can be on ground or in a big wide ocean.

God's words says he will come to the depths of the
sea to get you.

Surely goodness and mercy shall
follow us all the days of our lives.
Psalms 23:6

About the Author

Freda Harrison

She is a retired nurse. Her nursing was in the field of Alchemers, Cancer and prosperity, and wrote a book for caregivers of Alchemies called Hope, Keep tape alive. She is now running a non-profit where she works with addictions and a life crisis at New Horizon LIFE Coaching and enjoys it.